Tom Holland received a double first from Cambridge. He has adapted Homer, Herodotus, Thucydides and Virgil for BBC Radio. One of his earlier books, *Rubicon*, was shortlisted for the Samuel Johnson Prize and won the Hessell-Tiltman Prize for History 2004.

The Poison in
the Blood

Tom Holland

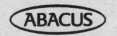

ABACUS

First published in Great Britain in May 2006 by Abacus

Copyright © Tom Holland 2006

The moral right of the author has been asserted.

A CIP catalogue record for this book
is available from the British Library.

ISBN-13: 978-0-349-11964-9
ISBN-10: 0-349-11964-3

Typeset by SX Composing DTP, Rayleigh, Essex

Printed and bound in Great Britain

Abacus
An imprint of
Time Warner Book Group UK
Brettenham House
Lancaster Place
London WC2E 7EN

www.twbg.co.uk

Cast of characters

Alcmena – mother of Heracles

Aphrodite – daughter of Zeus; the goddess of love

Athena – daughter of Zeus; the goddess of wisdom

Cronos – son of Sky and Mother Earth; father of Zeus

Dianeera – wife of Heracles

Helen – daughter of Zeus and the Queen of Sparta

Hera – wife of Zeus; Queen of the Heavens

Heracles – son of Zeus; world's greatest hero

Hermes – son of Zeus; the messenger of the gods

Iolus – boy who helped Heracles defeat the hydra; the brother of Dianeera

Odysseus – love rival of Philoctetes; husband of Penelope

Paris – Prince of Troy; lover of Yonani; kidnapper and lover of Helen

Penelope – Helen's cousin; wife of Odysseus

Philoctetes – goatherd who lit Heracles's funeral fire; future king

Yonani – goddess of the mountain; lover of Paris

Zeus – King of the Universe

ONE

THERE ONCE LIVED A goddess in a forest on a mountain. Her name was Yonani. She was wise and beautiful, but also very shy. She never climbed on the winds to Mount Olympus, where Zeus, the King of the Universe, had his palace. Yonani preferred trees to marble. She preferred grass and moss to gold. She would rather run with deer and speak to birds than feast with her fellow gods. On the mountain Yonani could be happy. On the mountain she could be alone.

Below the mountain there stretched a plain. A city named Troy stood on it. The King who ruled there was the richest man in the world, so nowhere had more towering battlements, or lovelier daughters, or braver sons. Bold as they were, however, the Trojans were afraid to visit Yonani's mountain. They never saw the goddess, but they knew that she was there. They did not wish to anger her, so they left her to herself.

Sometimes a shepherd might climb the mountain, if he had to, if a sheep were lost. But he would never stay after dark. No one would. Then, one night, when the Queen of Troy was pregnant, she had a terrible dream. In it, she gave birth . . . but not to a child. Instead, the Queen dreamed that she gave birth to fire. The flames leapt from her room. They set all the wide streets ablaze. The city's towers came crashing down. Troy was burned to the ground. The Queen woke up screaming. What had the dream meant? The priests knew and they told the Queen. The baby in her belly would prove the ruin of Troy. The Queen wept. The King held her in his arms . . . but he wept as well. Both knew what they had to do. When the baby was born, it was a beautiful boy. The King gave him to a shepherd who was told to take the baby to the top of the mountain and abandon him there to die. The shepherd left Troy. The Queen watched him go. Still she sobbed. She knew that she would never see her baby boy again.

Years passed. At the foot of the mountain, Troy grew richer still. Her ships sailed over all the seas. Her golden chariots raced across the plain. Her king fathered a host of brave princes. Meanwhile, in her forest, Yonani still lived alone. Then, one day, by a spring, she saw a man. He was young and very strong. The silver water shone on his shoulders as he swam. Yonani felt her heart rise into her mouth. The man turned and looked up at her from the spring. His blue eyes glittered. Yonani gasped. She thought she had never seen anyone so desirable – not even a god. Suddenly a longing for him came over her. She did not recognise her feelings at first, but then he stood and rose from the water, and she understood perfectly what she felt. She had discovered what it was to be in love.

Yonani was used to men feeling terror of her. The stranger, however, did not seem afraid. He fixed Yonani with a cool and easy gaze. His name, he told her, was Paris. He was a shepherd. He lived with his father and his mother at the foot of the mountain. He stepped out of the spring. Behind Yonani, leaves moved in a breeze. 'Beware,' they whispered in her ear. Yonani turned. She melted into the forest. As she vanished, as fast as the wind, she glanced back over her shoulder. Paris was still standing there.

The next day, Yonani returned to the spring. Paris came to find her. He was carrying a lamb.

'You are the goddess of the mountain,' he said. It was not a question, but a statement of fact.

Yonani nodded.

'They say you can heal anything you care to. They say you only have to see a sickness and at once you know the cure.' Paris paused. 'Is this the truth?'

Yonani nodded again. She still said nothing.

Paris held the lamb up to her. The creature's head was lolling. All its body was limp. 'Please,' he begged.

Yonani took the lamb. She laid her hand upon its fleece. And at once she knew what was wrong. 'A snake,' she said. 'It was by the river. The lamb went to drink and was bitten by a snake.'

'Can you heal him?' asked Paris.

Yonani laid her hand upon the lamb's head a second time. She closed her eyes. She listened to the clouds, to the breeze, to the sap rising in the trees. She felt a surge of power. It was like gold in her blood. She felt the lamb raise its head. She opened her eyes. The lamb began to struggle in her arms. She placed it down on the grass. 'It is cured,' she declared.

Paris smiled. 'Thank you.' He did not bow, as a mortal should to a goddess.

'Beware,' she heard from the leaves. This time, Yonani ignored the warning. She waited for Paris to take her in his arms. When he did, she let out a puzzled sigh. Then she met his lips. And with the kiss, all her puzzlement vanished away.

TWO

Yonani and Paris lived together. They were in love. Yonani showed Paris all the secrets of the mountain. She showed him how to talk to the animals. She showed him how to talk to the trees. She would still sometimes hear the leaves rustle. 'Beware,' they whispered. 'Beware.' Yonani ignored what they said. Her joy was too strong. She wanted her happiness with Paris to last for ever.

One day he lost a sheep and went to look for it. Yonani sat by the spring where she had first met him. Suddenly she saw a flash of gold reflected in the water. She looked up. The sky filled with light, then it was gone. The light had plunged into the forest. Yonani rose to her feet. She was afraid. She knew what the light had been: a god. But why had another god come to her forest? And where was Paris? Yonani's heart pounded. She began to run. As she ran, all the leaves began to whisper again: 'Beware.'

Ahead of her there was a parting in the trees. Yonani stopped in the shade of the trees. The clearing shimmered with a strange glow. Paris was standing in the middle of it, but he was not alone. A god was standing there, too. He was taller than Paris. On his head he wore a helmet with beating wings. His sandals had wings as well. In his hand he held a long pole. Two snakes were entwined around it. Yonani knew him at once. His names was Hermes. He was the messenger of Zeus.

From where she was hiding, Yonani could hear every word that was spoken.

'I have come from Olympus,' said Hermes. 'My father, Zeus, has sent me to find you. Here' – he held out something – 'take this.'

Yonani looked at what Hermes was holding. It was an apple. The apple was made of gold.

'This was given yesterday as a gift to Zeus,' said Hermes.

Yonani watched as Paris took it. There were words written on the apple. Paris read them aloud. '"For the fairest."' He frowned. '"For the fairest"? Who does that mean?'

Hermes smiled. 'That is what Zeus has ordered you to decide.'

'Why me?'

Hermes smiled again. 'Because who in the universe is fairer than the wife and the two daughters of Zeus? But which of those three is the most fair? Zeus does not wish to have to choose between his wife and his daughters. The apple can be given only to one. The losers would never forgive him.'

Paris turned pale. 'But why would they ever forgive me?'

Hermes didn't answer this question. He only smiled again.

'What if I refuse to award the apple?'

'Then Zeus will kill you.' Hermes shrugged. 'He will burn you up with a thunderbolt.'

Paris swallowed. 'So I have no choice.'

'It would seem not.'

As Hermes said this, a splendour filled the clearing. It was even brighter than it had been before. Paris cried out in pain, then held an arm up to his eyes. When he lowered it, a woman was standing in front of him. She was tall and regal. She wore a crown on her curling black hair. Her robes were purple. Her sandles were made of gold. 'I am Hera,' she said. 'I am the wife of Zeus. I am the Queen of the Heavens.'

Paris cried out in pain again, for Hera's beauty still hurt his eyes. But he could not stop looking at her.

'Give me the apple,' commanded Hera, 'and I will make you King of the World. You will lead great armies. You will win great victories. Everyone will bow and kiss your feet.' She held out her arm. Her fingers brushed Paris's head.

Paris brought his hands to his eyes. He fell to the ground in pain. When he looked up again, Hera had gone. In her place there was a second goddess. Her grey eyes were bright. She wore a helmet on her head. In her hand she held a spear. An owl sat on her shoulder. When Paris looked at her, he moaned. She, too, was so beautiful that her beauty hurt his eyes.

'I am Athena,' she said. 'I am the daughter of Zeus. I am the wisest of all the gods. Give me the apple, and you will share in my wisdom. You will know the secrets of the universe. Nothing will be hidden from you. You will see to the depths of the earth. You will see to the heights of the stars.' She held out her arm. Her fingers brushed Paris's head.

Paris brought his hands to his eyes. He fell to

the ground in pain. When he looked up again, Athena had gone. In her place was a third goddess. Her hair was of the purest gold. Her body was clothed in the sheerest silk. Around her waist she wore a belt of jewels. Where she trod, flowers sprung. Doves followed her. Her perfume filled the air. She was so beautiful that even Yonani had to blink. Paris could not stand to look at her. He fell to his knees. He pressed his face against the flowers that had bloomed around the goddess's feet.

'I am Aphrodite,' she whispered. Her voice was like a stirring of lust. Yonani heard Paris moan. 'I am the goddess of love. I do not promise you a crown. I do not promise you wisdom. But give me the apple, and I promise you something more. I promise you beauty. I promise you the love of the most beautiful woman in the world.'

At last, Paris dared to look up. 'Who is she?' he stammered.

'Her name is Helen,' answered Aphrodite. 'Her father is Zeus and her mother is Leda, the mortal Queen of Sparta, a city across the sea, in Greece. All the world desires her. But give me the apple, and Helen will be yours.'

Paris moaned again. 'I want her,' he said thickly.

'Then give me the apple.' Aphrodite held out her arm. Her fingers brushed Paris's head.

Paris continued to look at her. His grip tightened on the apple. He raised his hand.

'No!' cried Yonani.

Paris looked round. Hermes frowned. Aphrodite only laughed.

'No,' said Yonani again. She stepped out from the trees. 'Paris, you are mine. Do not do this. Do not leave me. You love me. You love me. Please.'

Paris looked at her. Then he looked down at the apple.

'You are a shepherd,' said Yonani. 'Helen is the daughter of a queen. How can you hope to win her?'

Aphrodite clapped her hands together. 'A shepherd? He is not a shepherd. He is a prince. The son of a king.'

Paris frowned in confusion. 'But my father is a shepherd.'

'No.' Aphrodite looked at Yonani with a smile that showed she'd won. 'Did you not realise? Paris is the same baby that the King of Troy

11

ordered to be left on the mountain. There he was found by a shepherd. But that shepherd is not his father.' She smoothed her fingers through Paris's hair. 'Give me the apple, and I will lead you to Troy. Your mother, the Queen, will fall into your arms. Your father, the King, will hail you as a Prince of Troy. Then you will sail to Greece. You will steal Helen from her husband and take the most beautiful woman in the world to your bed.'

'No!' cried Yonani.

But it was too late. Paris raised his hand. He gave the apple to Aphrodite. She clutched it to her breasts. There was a shimmering of light, and she was gone. All the gods had gone. All except for Yonani. She stood where she was. Then she watched Paris rise to his feet, leave the clearing, and start running through the trees, down the mountainside to Troy.

THREE

HE DID NOT RETURN. Yonani waited. Days passed, then weeks. Yonani felt her heart turning to stone. The mountain grew wintry with her misery. Snow settled upon the trees. The spring where Yonani had met Paris was covered by a sheet of ice. The flow of its waters froze. So did the flow of Yonani's tears. She sat alone on the bleak mountain. There was no warmth left in her heart.

Spring came at last. Yonani was disturbed by a shepherd. He was looking for a ewe. For a moment, she thought the shepherd was Paris – but he wasn't. He screamed when he saw Yonani and begged for mercy. Yonani seized him by the arm. He howled. She silenced him with a flash of her blazing eyes. Then she demanded to know the news from Troy.

The shepherd told her. Great things had happened. Everything Aphrodite had said had come true. Paris had been recognised by his parents, the King and Queen of Troy, as their long-lost son. In their love and shame, they had promised him anything. Paris had asked for a ship and had sailed on it to Greece. He had been welcomed there as a special guest by Menelaus, the King of Sparta. Helen, the Queen, the most beautiful woman in the world, had also welcomed Paris. He had captured her in the night and brought her back with him to Troy. She was there now, in Paris's bed. All of Troy was in love with Helen. They were dazzled by her beauty.

Yonani let the shepherd go. She felt as though her heart had cracked. She sped through the trees and reached the summit of the mountain. She looked at Troy far below her on the plain. Paris was there, somewhere within its walls, in bed with another woman. Yonani choked. For the first time, she cried. As she did so, she felt the ice in her heart turn to a fiery hatred.

Another year passed. Rumours of war reached Yonani. One day she climbed to the summit of her mountain again, and when she looked out to sea she saw a fleet of a thousand ships heading for Troy. When they got there, a great army of men wearing bronze pulled their ships on to the beach. Yonani knew who they were. They were the Greeks. They had come with Menelaus to claim back Helen. They built their camp on the beach. The Trojans came out from behind their walls to meet them. There was a great battle. Neither side won. The Trojans withdrew to their city, the Greeks back to their camp. The walls of Troy could not be brought down, but the Greeks did not go away.

They stayed in their camp for nine years, and for nine years the walls of Troy held firm. For nine years the Greeks and the Trojans fought. Sometimes Yonani would hear the din of battle drifting up to her through the trees. Sometimes she would see a dirty haze in the sky, as thousands of marching feet kicked up the dust of the plain. But the war never came to her forest. The Greeks, like the Trojans, were afraid of the goddess. They knew better than to climb up her mountain and risk her anger. Even the shepherds kept away now.

So Yonani had no news of Paris. She did not even know if he were dead or alive. Her hatred of him was as strong as ever – but so too was her love. She wanted him to suffer – but she wanted him to be safe. By now it was the tenth year of the war. It seemed to Yonani, watching the plain from her mountain, that the fighting was getting even worse. Sometimes the battle could not be seen for all the arrows. The sound of bronze hitting bronze made the horizon echo. Rivers flowed with blood. Yonani grew afraid.

Then, one day, she heard a crashing through the trees coming up the mountain. She cupped her ear. She stood frozen to the spot, startled. Mortals had dared to enter her forest. Her face darkened with anger. At the same time she felt a surge of excitement. Now she could find out what had happened to Paris. She moved like the wind to the spring where she had first met him. There she sat and listened to the water. She also listened to the crashing of the men coming up the mountain. They were making straight for her, as though they knew where to find her; as though someone were directing them to the very spot.

It had to be Paris. Yonani gazed through the trees and saw a group of men approaching her. They looked pale. When they saw her they lowered their eyes and began to shake. But still they climbed towards her and, as they drew nearer, Yonani saw they were carrying a stretcher.

She rose to her feet. 'Paris,' she called.

'He is dying,' answered one of the men carrying the stretcher. 'He asked to be brought to you. He said that only you could save him.'

Yonani's face darkened again. She stood where she was. She did not go down to meet the stretcher. She waited for it to be brought to her. The men carrying it stopped before her and lowered the stretcher.

Yonani looked down. There was Paris. His face was burning. It was covered with beads of sweat. He was tearing at his skin. It was as though his own blood were burning inside him. He wet his dry lips with his tongue. 'Yonani,' he gasped. 'Yonani.'

She did not answer.

'Please,' he begged. 'Heal me.'

'Why should I do that?'

'Because you can heal anything you care to. You have only to see a sickness and at once you know the cure. You think I have forgotten that?'

'I thought you had forgotten me.'

'No,' moaned Paris. His breath rattled. 'No, no, no . . .'

17

Yonani stooped and laid a hand on his forehead. It burned. She closed her eyes. She listened to the clouds, to the breeze, to the sap rising in the trees. She felt a surge of power. It was like gold in her blood. 'Poison,' she said. 'Poison on an arrow's tip.'

'Yes,' moaned Paris. 'There was an arrow . . .'

One of his attendants lifted the blanket that covered his leg. There was a thin scar on the thigh.

'There,' said Paris. 'An arrow. This morning. Just a graze.'

'But it was poisoned,' said Yonani. 'Just a graze, but it set the poison to work in your blood.'

'Then cure me!'

'Do you know what the poison is?' asked Yonani, laying a hand on Paris's forehead.

He struggled to sit up. 'No. Tell me.'

Yonani rose to her feet again. She looked down at Paris coldly. 'I know what the poison is,' she said. 'And I know where the arrow came from. Are you sure you wish me to tell you? Do you truly want to know the worst?'

Paris looked up at her desperately. He licked his lips and nodded. 'I want to know.'

18

'It is a long story,' answered Yonani. 'But I think you should have just enough time to hear it.'

And so she began her tale.

FOUR

IN THE BEGINNING, SAID Yonani, before there were men or gods, there was only one living thing in the universe. That was the Sky. Everything else was chaos. Infinite chaos. Chaos without end. Then, in the middle of the chaos, something took shape. This was Mother Earth. She spread and became solid. The Sky had been lonely for eternity. Now there was another living being alongside him in the universe. He fell on Mother Earth and embraced her. Not an inch of her body was left uncovered.

All the Sky could think of was sex. He had to have Mother Earth. He pumped his seed into her without rest. Mother Earth became pregnant. But she couldn't give birth. The Sky was still on top of her. Still he fucked her. Mother Earth became pregnant again. And again. And again. Soon her belly was filled with children. But none of them could escape. Mother Earth

20

groaned with the pain. She felt she would burst. Still the Sky continued to fill up her belly with seed.

At last, Mother Earth could bear it no longer. She spoke to her unborn children. 'Listen!' she said. 'Your father will never stop his rape of me. You will be prisoners inside my belly for ever. Something must be done. You must attack him, quickly!'

But her children were scared. They did not want to attack their father. They were afraid of what the Sky might do to them. However, one of the children overcame his fear. His name was Cronos. He made a sickle and sharpened the blade, then pushed his way through his mother's bulging womb. He swam through his father's flow of seed and reached for the Sky's testicles. He grabbed them in his hand. The Sky howled in agony. His cry filled the universe. Cronos tightened his grip. With his other hand he raised the sickle. Swish! The sickle came slicing down. The blade severed the Sky's testicles right through. He cried out in pain and finally pulled out of Mother Earth. He shrank from her as far as he could. He shrank to the limits of the universe. The Sky and Mother

Earth were separate at last. Their children could escape from their mother's belly. Out they came. They filled the earth and life began.

And Cronos? He held his father's testicles in his right hand, then flung them over his shoulder. They soared through the air before falling at last in a froth of blood and sperm. The blood and sperm bubbled and turned the earth where they fell into mud. Centuries passed, but they did not stop bubbling. And the mud and blood and sperm began to thicken into a soup. Then into a slime. Then into living flesh. At first it just beat and shook – a horrible, pulsing heart. Swamps stretched all around it. The liquid was poisonous. No one dared to enter it. No one disturbed the thing that was lurking in the swamp. More centuries passed; and the thing began to grow.

Meanwhile, in the world beyond the swamps, great events were taking place. Cronos had made himself the King of the Gods. He married his sister. Together, they had children. But Cronos was afraid. He was scared that one of these children would attack him, as he had attacked his father, the Sky. Whenever his sister gave birth to a son or daughter, he would swallow the child. His sister wept. She did not want Cronos to swallow all her children, so when she gave birth to her last baby, she hid him in a cave. When Cronos demanded the baby, she handed him a stone wrapped in a blanket. Cronos swallowed the stone. He did not know that the baby was still alive.

The baby's mother called him Zeus. Once he had grown up, he left the cave in which he had been hiding. He made a potion and swapped it for the wine that Cronos was drinking. The potion made Cronos vomit and up came the stone he had swallowed. Next came the children, Zeus's brothers and sisters, all of them still alive. They attacked their father. Cronos was flung into a pit of darkness. Zeus took his father's crown. With his brothers and sisters, he made his home on Mount Olympus. There he married his sister, Hera, and ruled as the King of the Gods.

More centuries passed. The rule of Zeus gave peace to the world. The wilderness was tamed. Fields were ploughed. Cities were built. Sometimes Zeus would walk around the world and admire the beauty of the women. If he desired one, he would take her. He was the King of the Universe, after all. He could do as he pleased. And sometimes one of these women would bear him a child.

One day, the gaze of Zeus fell upon the city of Argos. He stared into the King's palace, into the room where Alcmena, the King's wife, was having a bath. He felt a blaze of lust. He moved through the sky. He fell upon Alcmena, wrapped her in his arms and plunged deep. He spasmed and bellowed with the joy of it. He knew in that instant that Alcmena would bear him a son.

Back on Olympus, he told the other gods his news. Alcmena's son, he promised, would be the greatest hero who had ever lived. The other gods applauded. Only Hera narrowed her eyes. She felt a bitter pang of jealousy. When the child was born, he was named Heracles, in Hera's honour, but she still hated him. No sooner had Heracles been laid in his cradle than she sent two giant snakes to kill him. But Heracles only gurgled, and reached out for the snakes with his bare hands. He gripped their necks, his fingers tightened and he killed them both. He tossed away their bodies. And all the while he continued to gurgle and smile.

Heracles grew up to be incredibly strong. Everyone in Argos loved and admired him. Everyone was glad when he became their king. But Hera had other plans for him. She sent a fit of madness upon him and he went insane. He ran through the palace, frothing at the mouth. He reached for a dagger, and killed everyone in his path. He killed his own wife. He killed his own children. When the madness came to an end, he blinked and rubbed his eyes. He didn't know what he had done. When he found out, he threw himself to the ground in despair and tried to kill himself. His friends managed to stop him. Heracles's grief could not be stopped, however. After all, he had committed a terrible crime: he had murdered his family. How could he pay for it? He travelled to an oracle. Mortals who came to the oracle could ask for answers to their questions. The oracle told Heracles that he could no longer be the King of Argos. Instead, he would have to leave his palace and roam the world. His task would be to clear the world of all its monsters. Wherever they hid, Heracles would have to hunt them down. By doing this, he would pay for his crime. The spirits of his wife and his children would finally find their rest.

Heracles returned to Argos and told his people what the oracle had said. They wept and begged their king to stay, but Heracles refused. He laid down his crown and gave up almost everything he owned. The only things he kept were a sword, a bow and arrows, and a club. Then he headed off, to search the world for monsters. He had soon left Argos behind.

Meanwhile, in the swamps that stretched south of Argos, something was stirring. Something bred out of mud and sperm and blood. Something hungry for human flesh.

FIVE

SHEEP AND CATTLE BEGAN to vanish first. Then the shepherds and farmers who looked after them, men who lived alone, not the kind to be missed. Even so, the people of Argos began to whisper. They cast nervous eyes towards the swamps. The mists that rose from them had always seemed like poison. Now the shadow seemed to be spreading. The roads began to empty. Men locked their doors at night. Fear like the closeness of a muggy day spread over Argos.

Then, horror! A man rode from his village to the market at Argos. He sold what he had brought to sell. It was late by the time the market finished. The man spent the night in the city. In the morning he climbed on to his horse and made the journey back to his village. First, he smelled the stench, acrid and burning, but mixed with a sticky sweetness. Then he noticed the silence. Only an open door creaking in the breeze made any noise. The man rode into the village square and looked about. No one. He called out. No answer. He climbed down from his horse, crossed to his house and entered it. Then he screamed. There, on the floor, lay puddles of melted flesh and bone. His family. He could tell by the matted scraps of hair. But of their human form nothing was left. Something had torn them to shreds. Something that had dissolved the few remains into sludge. All across the village there were these scenes of murder. No one had been spared. Everywhere there rose the acrid stench, and the ground itself seemed scorched.

The poor man was dazed with shock and misery. Nevertheless, he jumped on to his horse and galloped back to Argos. He told everyone what he had seen. The new King ordered his men to go to the village. When they arrived, they looked around for clues. They soon found a trail leading from the village. A monster wider than a house appeared to have left it. The smell of acid rose from the tracks. Drops of something like poison had fallen on the grass along the way and burned up the soil. The King's men followed the trail until it reached the edge of the swamp. The water was bubbling. No one dared to go any further. Instead, they hurried back to the King and told him what they had found.

The next day, another village was found empty, save for the remains of melted human flesh. Again, a monstrous trail led from the village to the swamp. The King was in despair. He offered a reward to any man who would dare to enter the swamp. No one accepted it. Everyone was too afraid. People from the villages began to crowd into Argos and the city became full. Everyone stood on the streets and in the market place. They talked about the monster in the swamp. Then they talked about Heracles. They all agreed that he was the only man who could save them. But no one knew where he was. He had gone out into the world to fight monsters – never knowing that there was one on his own doorstep. Messengers were sent to find him. The people of Argos waited and prayed to the gods that Heracles would be found. Days passed. Then, at last, he came.

He was wearing a lion's hide. The forelegs hung over his shoulders. The hind legs covered his own. The mane covered the back of his head and neck. The teeth protected his forehead. When the King asked where the lion hide had come from, Heracles told him the story.

He had travelled, he said, from Argos to Nemea. He had heared that the people of Nemea were being hunted by a giant lion. Heracles left Nemea and took the road that led into the mountains where the lion's cave was. When Heracles arrived at the cave, he saw human bones around the opening. He gave a great war-cry and the lion came padding out. It was a giant. When it roared, Heracles felt the blast of its breath directly into his face. The breath stank of meat. The lion leapt and Heracles shot at it with his bow. But the arrow bounced harmlessly off the lion's side. The lion kept coming forward, and so Heracles swerved out of its way. He pulled out his sword and struck the neck of the lion. The sword shattered into tiny fragments. The lion swiped at him with its claws. Heracles ducked while reaching for his club. He smashed it on to the lion's head with no effect, so he threw the club away. He reached for the lion's neck with his bare hands and pressed his fingers tight around its throat. The lion roared. Clinging to one another,

Heracles and the lion rolled down the mountainside. Heracles continued to squeeze the lion's throat. Tighter and tighter his fingers gripped. The lion began to choke. With one last spasm, its body finally fell still. Heracles rose to his feet. Then he realised the lion's hide was stronger than any armour. He wanted it for himself, and so he tried to skin the carcass, but he couldn't cut through the hide. In the end, he used the lion's own claws to slice it off. After cleaning the hide, he had tied it over his shoulders.

That was the story, and everyone who heard it felt a sudden surge of relief. They all began to shout, begging Heracles to go to the swamps and kill whatever lay lurking there.

Heracles knew his duty and promised that he would go to the swamps at once. He set out on the road that led to them. As he left, the people of Argos watched him from the city walls. Only one of them dared to follow: a young boy named Iolus. He dreamed of being a hero, and he was ashamed that no one else in Argos was brave enough to accompany Heracles. Of course, when Heracles looked round and saw the young boy following him, he was angry. He

31

ordered Iolus to return to his mother. Iolus refused. Instead, he scampered ahead of Heracles down a path that led to the swamps. There, by the side of the water, was a boat.

'Let me row you,' said Iolus. 'How else will you be able to get into the swamp?'

Heracles stepped into the boat. 'Give me the oars,' he said, 'and go back to your mother.'

'I won't,' said Iolus.

Heracles frowned. He reached for the oars. Iolus stepped backwards. At that moment, a wave hit the boat and Heracles and Iolus almost fell over. The wave washed them further into the bubbling waters of the swamp.

'Wha . . . what was that?' stammered Iolus.

Heracles held up a hand. 'Sssssshhhh.' He pointed. In the distance, something huge was slipping through the reeds. Then, with a splash, it vanished into a fresh expanse of water. A new wave came rushing towards the boat and rocked it so that Heracles and Iolus almost fell over again. The boat drifted further into the swamp.

'What was it?' asked Iolus again.

'Trouble,' said Heracles. He took an arrow from his quiver and placed it in his bow. Then he turned to Iolus and gestured with his head. There was no talk of sending Iolus back to his mother now. Iolus picked up the oars and began to row. The boat slipped through the water. The mist thickened. Not a sound could be heard except the splashing of the oars. Heracles crouched. His knuckles whitened around his bow. Iolus continued to row but it was becoming harder as the water seemed to thicken. He looked down at the swamp: it was green and purple and red. It bubbled with lazy plops. Then, suddenly, the oar hit something. He peered over the side and screamed. There, in the water, was a bobbing, half-eaten corpse. Iolus looked around. Corpses were everywhere. The swamp was a soup of melting corpses. Iolus screamed again.

At that moment, something monstrous loomed out of the mist.

SIX

AT FIRST THERE WAS only a single neck. It rose up high, like a snake's. Its eyes were narrow with hunger. It had orange and scarlet frills around its neck. Its mouth snarled open. Its teeth were razor sharp. Drool dripped from them. When the drool landed in the water, it hissed. When it landed on mud or rushes, it burned them. The neck coiled and twisted. The head darted. The jaws were open wide. It spat poison at the boat. Iolus had to row frantically to avoid it. The boat rocked. Heracles stumbled. The water hissed and boiled where the monster's poison splashed.

Heracles pulled back the string of his bow. He aimed. He fired. The arrow sang as it flew. It thudded into the open mouth of the monster, which bellowed in pain. Its blood was black. It spurted out in a thick flood from between the monster's jaws. It splashed into the water. Again the water boiled.

'You killed it!' shouted Iolus. 'You killed it!'

'No,' replied Heracles. 'Look.' He pointed.

Iolus stared. Something seemed to be moving beneath the water. Coils, twisting and turning. 'More snakes?' he yelled in terror.

Heracles shook his head. He strung another arrow and gritted his teeth. 'A hydra,' he whispered. 'It is a hydra. A hydra with a hundred necks.'

Suddenly a second head rose from the depths. Its neck arched high above the boat. It was followed by a third. Then a fourth, a fifth, a sixth. Heracles's bow hummed. Arrow after arrow flew. But heads rose from the swamp faster than Heracles could shoot them; faster than Iolus could count them as well. Perhaps there were a hundred, he thought in terror. Perhaps more. The necks coiled and seethed and darted forwards and back. Arrows had hit many of them, but not all. And even those that Heracles had struck with an arrow continued to twitch and snap.

'Over there!' yelled Heracles. He pointed to an island covered with reeds. 'Row me over there!'

Iolus obeyed. As the boat sped towards the

island, the hydra followed. The water became more shallow. Iolus could see the monster's body rising from the swamp. It was vast. Its scales glittered like garnets. Its heart was a loathsome, pounding, quivering thing. It heaved itself through the mud. Its necks coiled in pursuit of Heracles and Iolus. Its heads could smell blood. They were hungry for human flesh, driven mad by the craving for it.

The boat came to a halt among the reeds and mud flats. Heracles dropped his bow and reached for his sword. Two of the hydra's heads came slavering down towards him. Heracles's sword sliced twice, cutting through scales, flesh and bone. The two heads dropped like stones into the mud. Heracles jumped out of the boat and yelled at Iolus to row to safety. Iolus pulled on the oars and the boat drifted away from the island. Meanwhile, Heracles was stepping through the reeds. Another pair of jaws snapped at him. He turned. His sword cut through the air. A flash of bronze, then a spray of black blood. It spattered Heracles, but the poison could not burn through the lion's skin. A third head dropped into the mud.

Heracles reached dry land and stood with his

sword at the ready. The hydra attacked him again, necks coiling, jaws snapping. Heracles sliced at them. His arm moved so fast that Iolus could not see the sword as it did its work. Heads thudded to the ground all around Heracles as he fought. But the hydra did not withdraw. It pressed on with its attack. There seemed no limit to its number of heads. Iolus watched the battle from the boat and began to worry that Heracles would grow tired.

He rowed around to the far side of the island. The boat's prow rested on a mud bank and Iolus lowered his oars. He caught his breath and looked again at the fight. This time he felt a surge of relief. Heracles was fighting as well as ever while the hydra was slowing. Heads were still spitting and snapping, but they were outnumbered now by stumps. Slice, slice, slice. More heads dropped among the reeds. Iolus counted those that were left: no more than twenty. Still Heracles fought. Fifteen heads left. Then ten.

Suddenly Iolus frowned. Something strange was happening. He rubbed his eyes. There seemed to be more heads than there had been a moment before. He counted them again.

Fifteen. Twenty. Iolus rose to his feet and stared at the hydra's bleeding stumps. They were all twitching and growing before his eyes. The bleeding flesh of the stumps was healing. From one, a pair of eyes appeared. Then a set of jaws. The mouth opened. A hissing. A scarlet frill opened out behind the head. A slice of Heracles's sword and it was sent flying, but in the meantime, more heads were reappearing. No matter how fast Heracles beheaded them, more grew back to take their place.

Iolus shouted out what he had seen. He heard Heracles swear loudly. The heads were growing back faster and faster. Heracles began to retreat. Iolus picked up the oars. As Heracles withdrew across the island, the hydra heaved itself on to the dry land. This slowed it down and Heracles took his chance. He turned and ran across the island. He jumped into the boat. 'Pull away,' he yelled. 'Get us out of this swamp!' He reached for his bow and shot arrows at the hydra, which cried out in pain. But it still kept following them. As Iolus rowed, he despaired. The hydra could not be beaten. Heracles had failed.

SEVEN

OR HAD HE?

Jumping out of the boat as it reached dry land, Heracles did not seem like a beaten man. 'Quick,' he ordered. 'Find dry wood. Anything that will burn. Make a fire.'

Iolus wanted to ask why, but he knew there was no time. He did as Heracles had instructed. Minutes passed. From the swamp, Iolus heard the hissing of the hydra's heads. He looked round. The monster was getting nearer. Iolus grabbed branches, pulled up bushes and gathered grass. He made a pile of the wood. Behind him, he heard the twang of Heracles's bow. The hydra shrieked. Iolus looked round again. Heracles was firing arrows at the monster. For now, he was holding it at bay. But for how much longer? Iolus noticed that his hands were shaking. He picked up lighting flints and tried to strike a spark. Nothing. He swore. Still his hands shook. He breathed in deeply and tried again. This time, he had better luck. The spark lit the kindling. The day was hot and the wood was dry. Within a few minutes, the fire was blazing. Heracles glanced round and smiled. 'Good lad!' he cried.

'Watch out!' screamed Iolus.

Heracles spun on his heel. The open jaws of three of the hydra's heads were almost on him. With a single movement, Heracles drew his sword, then swung it through the air. The three heads went flying. As they did so, Heracles turned and ran. Not pausing, he reached for a tree trunk that was lying on the ground. Iolus had never even thought to try to move it. The trunk had looked too heavy. But Heracles picked it up easily. His muscles bulged. Sweat glistened on them. He was beside the fire now and shoved the trunk into the flames. As he did so, he looked over his shoulder. The hydra was drawing near. Heracles pulled the flaming tree trunk from the fire. He gripped it in his left hand. With his right, he lifted his sword. The hydra attacked and Heracles swung his sword. A head went flying. No sooner had it done so than Heracles was lifting the burning tree trunk. He laid the tip on the hydra's stump. The hundred other heads all shook and screamed with the pain. A smell of scorched flesh made Iolus want to vomit. Heracles withdrew the burning tree trunk. The stump was still. No head grew back.

Now the battle grew truly terrible. The hydra knew for the first time that it was in a struggle to the death. Its necks coiled around Heracles's legs, his body, his arms. But Heracles was too strong. He trampled the necks underfoot. He slashed and cut with his sword. Whenever he sent a head flying, he would burn the twitching stump. As ever more of its heads were lopped off, the hydra turned and tried to flee. But Heracles followed it. The hunter had become the hunted. Iolus ran in his master's footsteps and jumped into the boat after Heracles. He pulled on the oars and rowed after the hydra, into the depths of the swamp. At last, in the black poison of its lair, the hydra stopped retreating. The battle began again. But the hydra was weakening fast now. Finally, there was only one head left. Heracles slashed at it. For a long time he kept the burning tree trunk pressed against the severed neck. At last he withdrew it. The neck jerked, then was still.

Heracles leaned on his sword and inhaled deeply. He pushed back the head of his lion's skin. He wiped the sweat from his brow.

'You did it,' said Iolus. 'You did it!'

Heracles smiled. 'Of course. Did you ever doubt I would?'

Iolus blushed.

Heracles laughed, then paused and angled his head. 'What is that?' he said.

Iolus listened and heard a pulsing, a throbbing. He frowned and looked at the hydra. The noise seemed to be coming from its corpse. Or was it a corpse? Iolus took a nervous step nearer to it and pointed. 'Look,' he gasped. 'The heart.'

It was still beating. Heracles stepped up to it and laid his hand on the quivering, jerking scales. He thought for a moment, then he turned. 'Row back across the swamp,' he ordered. 'Look for my arrows. Find as many as you can. Then bring them to me. I will be waiting here.'

Iolus did as Heracles had instructed. It was horrible work. The heads of the hydra had already started to rot. Flies attracted by their smell lay dead in piles. The poison of the blood had killed them. Iolus realised he had to be careful with the arrows, so he took his time pulling them free from the stinking flesh and returning them to the quiver. It was late when he rowed back to Heracles: the sun was sinking in the west. A cloud of black smoke, rising from where Heracles stood, hid it from view. It was greasy and smelled of flesh. As Iolus reached the hydra's lair, he realised that his master had made a bonfire of the monster's heads. He handed Heracles the arrows.

Heracles thanked him, then crossed to the hydra's corpse. He drew his sword. 'Stand well back,' he said.

'What are you doing?' asked Iolus.

Heracles answered by raising his sword above his head. He aimed at the hydra's pulsing heart and brought the sword down hard. Heracles drove the blade deep into the heart and black blood began to froth out in a flood. Iolus shrunk back. The blood was burning whatever it touched. Heracles waited for the pulsing to subside, then he pulled his arrows from the quiver. He knelt down and, one by one, dipped the tips of the arrows into the hydra's blood. When he had finished, he carefully returned them to the quiver.

43

'A deadly weapon,' said Iolus.

Heracles nodded as he climbed into the boat. Iolus joined him. Together, they made their way back across the swamp.

And so ended the adventure of the hydra.

EIGHT

BUT HERACLES'S MONSTER-KILLING would continue. The hero roamed the world and fought with giant birds that had beaks and claws of bronze. He fought with giant bulls that breathed out fire. He fought with the three-headed dog that guarded the gates of the Underworld. Nothing could defeat him. He became what Zeus, his father, had promised he would be: the greatest hero who had ever lived.

But he would always return to Argos. When he came back, he would stay with Iolus since he had no home of his own. As he grew older, he became increasingly sad about this. Iolus had a wife and children. When Heracles saw them, it reminded him that he had none of his own. It reminded him of his madness. It reminded him of his crime.

Iolus had a young sister called Dianeera. She was extremely beautiful and Heracles was very fond of her. She lived with Iolus as she had no husband. One day, Heracles asked Iolus why she had never married. Iolus laughed. 'Haven't you guessed?' he asked.

Heracles frowned. He was puzzled.

'Ask her,' said Iolus.

Heracles did so. Dianeera blushed and covered her face with a veil before running away. Heracles watched her go. He thought how pretty her ankles were. He remembered how lovely she had looked as she had blushed. Suddenly he understood.

They were married a month later. For a year, Heracles lived with his new bride and did not go on any adventures. Then a message came for him. It told of a monster in a country far away. Heracles was needed so he picked up his club, tied on his lion's skin, and slung his bow and poisoned arrows over his shoulders. He kissed Dianeera goodbye, then he left.

He was away for a while year. When he finally returned to Argos, he stayed for a couple of months, but then he left again. This time he was away for ten months. And so it went on. Dianeera grew desperate. She begged Heracles not to leave. She begged him to spend more time with her. But Heracles always shook his head. He was needed, he explained. It was his duty. 'But why?' asked Dianeera. Heracles fell silent. Dianeera pressed him. Finally, Heracles told her about his first family, about how he had killed them all in his madness, about the order that the oracle had given him. Dianeera had not known any of this. She walked to their bedroom, lay down on their bed and sobbed.

Later that night, she told Heracles that she wanted to go with him on his next adventure. At first, Heracles laughed, but when he saw that she was serious, he shook his head. Dianeera insisted but still Heracles refused. They argued. The next day, when Dianeera was at the market, Heracles left Argos. Dianeera returned home to find the house empty. She called for Heracles but there was only silence. She quickly packed, loaded her bags on to a horse, then led the horse round to Iolus's house. She asked him where Heracles had gone. Iolus was surprised that she did not know. He told her: Heracles was heading for Thessaly.

'Where is Thessaly?' asked Dianeera.

'It is far to the north,' replied her brother.

'What is it like?'

'It is wild and savage, full of strange monsters. Just be thankful you will never visit it.'

Dianeera smiled a twisted smile. Without another word, she turned and left. She climbed back on to her horse and squeezed her thighs against its sides. The horse clattered down the street that led to the city gates. Dianeera asked the way to Thessaly and a guard pointed. Dianeera rode hard for three days.

On the fourth day, she saw steep and rugged mountains ahead of her. Thessaly. She rode through the night on the empty road. Only in the morning did she see someone ahead of her, striding fast. He carried a club. He had a bow and arrows slung over his shoulder. He wore a lion's skin on his back.

It was Heracles, of course. He was furious. He would not talk to his wife. But nor did he send her back. Instead, the two of them continued on their way together into the mountains. Soon they heard a crashing and a roaring coming from ahead of them. Heracles laid a hand on his wife's thigh and looked up at her. For the first time he spoke. 'Now we have a problem,' he said. He helped her down from the horse and led her round a curve of the mountain road.

Then he pointed. Ahead of them was a river. Spray boiled. The current surged. The opposite bank was in the far distance. 'Your horse will never make it,' said Heracles. 'And I am nervous, if I carry you, that I might lose my footing. One slip, and you would be swept away, dashed to pieces on the rocks. You cannot go on. You must make your way back to Argos.'

Dianeera stared at the river helplessly. She twisted a curl of hair around her finger. She did not know what to say. At that very moment, she heard a clopping of hooves behind her.

'Perhaps', said a voice, 'I might be of some help.'

NINE

DIANEERA SPUN ROUND AND gasped in amazement. The voice had come from only half a man. From his hips upwards he was human: he had a curling beard, pointed ears and hair all over his body. Below his hips, however, he was a horse: black and glossy, with a swishing tail. He bowed, and as he did so his front hooves clopped again on the rocks. 'I am Nessus,' said the horse–man. 'I am the keeper of this ford. I help anyone who wishes to cross the river.'

Dianeera thanked him, then she saw that her husband was staring at Nessus with narrowed eyes. She wondered why.

'Very well,' said Heracles, after a long pause. 'If you could take my wife on your back, I would be very grateful.'

Nessus bowed again and gave a polite sweep with his hand. 'After you.'

'No.' Heracles reached for Dianeera. 'After

you.' He lifted up his wife and placed her on Nessus's back.

Dianeera wrapped her arms tightly around the horse–man's body and looked down nervously at Heracles.

'I am watching you,' he said. As he did so, he reached for his bow and unslung it from his back. He leaned on it, still staring at Nessus. 'I am watching you both.'

Nessus flared his nostrils, and tossed his head. With a clattering of hooves he was away. He hurried over the rocks that led down to the river and plunged into the water. Dianeera gasped. The water was freezing and she could feel the currents tugging at her. She clung to Nessus for dear life, and she looked over her shoulder to see Heracles starting to cross the river. He was holding his bow high above him. He did not slip, but it was slow going for him. Nessus was much faster. Soon he had reached midway across the river. The noise was deafening. The spray shimmered and formed rainbows. The currents eddied and swirled. Dianeera clung even more tightly to Nessus, threading her fingers through the curling hair on his chest. Suddenly she felt him move even faster. He was

51

now past the worst and began to canter through the shallows. He clattered up on to dry land but did not slow down.

'Wait,' cried Dianeera. 'We must wait for Heracles!'

Nessus laughed. His canter turned into a gallop.

'Stop!' shouted Dianeera. She looked over her shoulder: Heracles was still only halfway across the river. She screamed and let go of Nessus, ready to jump off his back. But as she prepared to leap, Nessus reached for her. She felt his strong arm squeeze her. He pulled her off his back and his long nails dug deep into her flesh as she struggled. He wrapped his arms around her. She tried to break free, but he only laughed again. 'Heracles!' she screamed, but Nessus silenced her with a kiss. His rough lips bruised hers. The bristles of his beard scratched her chin. Still he galloped.

Dianeera screamed. Her eyes wide, she stared over Nessus's shoulder. Heracles was far away now, still in the middle of the river. But he was drawing back his bowstring. Then the arrow flew. Dianeera tried to cry out again, but Nessus was still kissing her, even as the arrow ripped into his back. Now it was Nessus's turn to scream. He stumbled and let go of Dianeera. She fell to the ground. As Nessus fell too, she rolled over and over. From behind her, she heard a crash and looked round. Nessus lay twitching in the dusk. He was pulling at his skin with his long nails. It was as though he wanted to rip it off. He roared in agony.

Dianeera rose to her feet and dusted herself down. She felt so bruised and dazed that she did not know what to do next.

'Dianeera.' Nessus's voice was hoarse and rattling. 'Dianeera, I am dying.'

She looked at him. 'Am I meant to feel sorry for you? You would have raped me. Death is all you deserve.'

Nessus wheezed and choked. He nodded his head. 'And I am sorry for it,' he gasped. 'Please, before I die, accept my apologies.'

Dianeera stared at him helplessly. She looked around. A mountain spring was bubbling near by. She crossed to it, crouched down and cupped her hands. She brought Nessus some water. He drank it greedily. When he had finished, he looked up at her with gratitude.

'Come closer,' he whispered, beckoning feebly. 'There is something I must tell you.'

Dianeera frowned at him with suspicion.

'Please. It is for your own good.'

Dianeera knelt down beside him.

'Listen,' wheezed Nessus. 'I have seen . . . your husband . . . If you ever . . .' He gasped for breath and swallowed. He tried again. 'If you ever . . .'

'What?' demanded Dianeera. 'What are you talking about?'

'If you ever feel . . . your husband . . . that his love for you . . . that his love for you is fading . . .'

Dianeera wanted to ask why that would ever happen, but she did not. She kept silent. She kept listening.

'Take a bottle . . . fill it with my blood . . . I tried to rape you for love . . . Now I die for love . . . My blood . . . is magical.'

'How? How?'

'A love charm.' Nessus smiled feebly. His breath was fading. 'Smear it on a robe . . . give it to your husband . . .' His eyelids fluttered, then closed. 'He will love you again.' A long, rattling gasp, then silence.

Dianeera laid her hand on Nessus's heart. It was still. She rose to her feet and looked to the river. Heracles had reached the shallows. He was almost on dry land. Quickly, Dianeera took a water bottle that was hanging from her belt and crouched down beside Nessus again. She held up his hand, slit his wrist with the arrow point and decanted his blood into the bottle. Then she stoppered it and hung it again from her belt.

Heracles walked up behind Dianeera, who turned. He took her in his arms and kissed her. Dianeera wrapped her arms around his shoulders. For a long while they embraced in silence. When Heracles finally let her go, Dianeera still held her tongue.

TEN

SHE HUGGED HER SECRET to herself.

Over the years that followed, she gave Heracles many children, and she lived happily with them in Argos. But she did not travel with her husband again – and he was away more and more. Sometimes, he would be gone for years at a time. Dianeera, left alone in Argos, would remember Nessus's words. 'If you ever feel that your husband's love for you is fading . . .' She could hear it ringing in her ears: Nessus's dying promise. At such moments, Dianeera would go to the cabinet where she kept the bottle filled with his blood. She would take it out, cup it in her hands, press it to her breasts. The love-charm.

On one of his trips, Heracles was away for five long years. Dianeera could feel herself growing old. When Heracles returned at last to Argos, his hair was grey, but he seemed as strong and fit as ever. He hugged Dianeera, kissed her, smiled and laughed and joked. But Dianeera did not smile. She rested her cheek on his chest and stayed there for a long while, listening to the beating of her husband's heart. Then she turned and left him. She went to their bedroom and looked in a mirror. She traced the lines on her face and touched the white hairs on her head. She crossed to her cabinet and removed a beautiful robe. She had bought it in the market place. It was embroidered with reds, purples and golden thread. Dianeera laid it out on the bed, returned to the cabinet and reached for the bottle filled with the love charm. She paused for a moment, standing beside the bed, then she uncorked the bottle and poured the love charm over the inside of the robe. Nessus's blood seeped into the fabric. Dianeera folded the robe neatly and called out to her maids to draw Heracles a bath. When he stepped out of it, she dried him herself. Then, as he stood naked, she presented him with the robe, holding it open for him. He pulled it on, wrapped it tight around his body, fastened it with a belt. Then, suddenly, he screamed.

He began tugging at the robe, trying to tear it off, but the fabric was already melting into his body. When he pulled at the robe, he was pulling at his own stomach. Bloody scraps of bubbling flesh dripped from his fingers. He stared at Dianeera with wide eyes. 'What have you done?' he cried. 'You have destroyed me! I am being eaten by the hydra's blood!'

'No,' sobbed Dianeera. 'No! It is to make you love me again!'

But Heracles was not listening. He was already running out of the house, out of the city. He was running for the mountains. Snow lay high on the peaks. All that Heracles could think of as he burned was to roll and roll in the snow.

Dianeera watched him go, then she returned to the bedroom. She took a cord from her gown made a noose, then tied the other end to a beam. She stood on a chair, slipped the noose over her neck and kicked away the chair. As she slowly throttled herself, the tears flowed down her cheeks and dropped to the floor.

Meanwhile, Heracles was also ready for death. He had reached the mountaintop, but the snow had done nothing to cool his body. As his flesh melted and dripped from his bones, he knew that his end had come. But he also knew that he would never truly die. He was the son of Zeus, and he was the greatest hero of all. If his mortal body were consumed by flames, then his spirit would climb to the heavens. He would live on as a god. In a frenzy, he began gathering wood. He gasped with agony as he worked, but he did not stop once for breath as he built a giant funeral fire. All around him, shepherds gathered to watch. When Heracles had finished, he climbed to the top of the mound of wood, lay down and called out to the shepherds. He ordered them to light the fire. They refused. The thought of killing Heracles was too awful to think about. Heracles roared at them to obey him, but all the shepherds disappeared down the mountainside. And still the poison bubbled and hissed and burned.

Some time later, a boy came walking by, herding goats. Heracles raised his head feebly and called out to the boy. He begged him to light the fire.

The boy looked up at the hero with wide eyes. He shook his head.

'What is your name?' asked Heracles.

'Philoctetes,' answered the boy.

'Then listen to me, Philoctetes,' said Heracles.

'Light the pyre, and I will give you a great gift. You may have my bow and my poisoned arrows. They are the deadliest weapons in the world. The boy who owns them will grow up to be a hero. Would you like that, Philoctetes? To grow up a hero? Or are you content to remain a goatherd all your life?'

The boy paused, but not for long. He scrambled to the top of the pyre and looked down at the dying hero. He saw how Heracles's flesh boiled and bubbled like a lava pool. He looked at the bow and arrows and saw how the great bow curved, how the tips of the deadly arrows glinted in the sun. He reached down and picked up the bow and arrows. He carried them with him as he clambered back down the mountain of wood and stood by its side. Then he took his lighting flints out of his pouch and struck a spark. Flames licked and curled around the wood of Heracles's funeral fire.

Within minutes, the blaze was raging. Philoctetes stepped back. The heat was holding him back like a wind. He could not make out the body of Heracles through the smoke but he heard a cry. It soared and echoed, then fell away. As it stilled to silence, Philoctetes saw the smoke form into the silver outline of a chariot. Ten prancing horses made of fire rose into the sky, and standing in the chariot was Heracles. His limbs were healed. His body was repaired. Light like a crown blazed from his head. He shook the reins of his chariot and the horses pawed at the sky. Up they soared, then wheeled and sped on their way to Olympus. Eventually they vanished, leaving only the black smoke. The flames coiled and raged. Sparks flew.

Philoctetes, watching until only ashes were left, smoothed his fingers up and down the bow, and knew that it was his.

ELEVEN

HE DID NOT STAY a goatherd for long. Just as
Heracles had promised it would, the great
bow made him famous. The poisoned arrows
continued to kill many monsters, and
Philoctetes became the greatest archer of his
day. He was adopted by his city's king, and
named a prince. When the King died,
Philoctetes took the crown. The boy who had
been a goatherd now sat on a royal throne.

One day, he was paid a visit by the king of a
nearby city called Sparta. He had his daughter
with him. Her name was Helen. Philoctetes
thought that she was the most beautiful girl he
had ever seen. She was so perfect that he
couldn't speak. At last, he found his tongue, but
he remained too shy to make any sense.
Fortunately, Helen was not the only princess to
have travelled with her father. Her cousin,
Penelope, had also come to visit Philoctetes.
She was beautiful, too, although not as beauti-

ful as Helen. Philoctetes found it much easier to talk to her, and when she left to return to Sparta he missed her terribly.

A few months later, strange news reached him. It was reported that princes from all over Greece were travelling to Sparta. They were all madly in love with Helen and wanted her as their bride. They were camped out in her father's palace, refusing to leave. Philoctetes decided that he would travel to Sparta as well. But he did not want Helen as his queen. His heart was set on Penelope.

When he arrived at Sparta, however, he found to his horror that there was another prince with the same idea. His name was Odysseus. He came from Ithaca, an island as tiny as it was poor. Philoctetes assumed that such a lowly prince was little threat to him, but he was wrong. Odysseus may not have been rich, but he was clever. Indeed, no one in the world was more cunning or ruthless.

Odysseus was determined to remove Philoctetes as a rival, so he went to see Helen's father. The King of Sparta was in a nervous state. He was upset to find himself with so many rival princes in his palace, thinking that the rejected suitors might cause trouble if he were forced to choose one of them as Helen's husband. Odysseus claimed to have a solution to the dilemma, but he told the king he would reveal it only if he were first given the hand of Penelope. The King of Sparta quickly agreed that he would. Odysseus whispered in his ear: 'Make all the princes swear an oath. Get them to promise upon the gods that they will accept Helen's choice of husband. Then, get them to promise that they will go to war with anyone who attempts to steal her away. An insult to Helen's husband must be regarded as an insult to the whole of Greece. Then, when everyone has sworn this oath, get the princes to stand in a circle, place Helen in the middle of it, blindfold her, spin her round, and order her to walk forwards with her arms outstretched. The first prince she touches will be her husband. That way, the choice will not have been yours. The gods will have made it for you.'

The King of Sparta decided this was an excellent plan and did exactly as Odysseus had advised. All the princes accepted his proposal, swore an oath that they would go to war with anyone who stole Helen from the man chosen to be her husband, then stood in a circle. Helen was led into the centre of the circle, blindfolded and spun round. Then she glided forwards with her arms outstretched. The first man she touched was Menelaus and the two were duly proclaimed husband and wife.

Of course, Menelaus was not the only prince to have won himself a bride. Odysseus, when he went home to Ithaca, took Penelope with him to be his queen.

Philoctetes went home alone. And just as there was poison on the heads of his arrows, now there was poison in his heart, too.

TWELVE

AT THIS POINT, YONANI paused in her story and looked down at Paris. His face was waxy. Bubbles of sweat beaded his grey skin. He twitched and turned. He plucked at his skin with his nails.

'Well?' asked Yonani. 'What do you think? Can jealousy be a worse poison than the venom currently boiling in your blood?'

Paris made a curious sound, midway between a sob and a laugh. 'It is hardly for me to say,' he gasped.

'No,' said Yonani coldly. 'It is not.' She paused again and listened to the faint sound of the battle on the plain far below. 'Philoctetes and his arrows; his deadly, poisoned arrows.' She crouched beside Paris, laid her cool fingers briefly on his burning cheek, then shook her head in mock-concern. 'Goodness me, you are on fire.' She rose to her feet again. 'Shall I tell you, *Prince Paris*, how it was that Philoctetes came to Troy?'

Paris did not answer. Perhaps he had been silenced by the bitterness of Yonani's tone. But he kept his eyes fixed on her and listened with pained attention as the goddess continued her tale.

'It was you', Yonani told him, 'you who brought Philoctetes here.'

Paris moaned, because he could hardly deny the charge. It was indeed his abduction of Helen that had brought Philoctetes, and all the other Greeks, to Troy. For no sooner had Menelaus learned that his wife had been kidnapped than he was vowing a terrible revenge. He sent news of the outrage to every city in Greece, reminding the princes of their oath. He called them to war with Troy. Most came willingly; a few were less happy about it.

Odysseus, for instance, only just married himself, had no wish to leave Penelope. He had his servants report that he had gone mad. Menelaus believed him, but Philoctetes did not. He told Menelaus that he would make sure that Odysseus came to Troy. He travelled to Ithaca and arrived at Odysseus's palace. There he found Penelope in tears. 'How am I going to bring up my son,' she sobbed, 'when his father has gone insane?' She showed Philoctetes her baby. The sight of the boy was like a blade through Philoctetes's heart. Penelope hugged the baby to her breast. 'He needs a father; a father who is sane.'

'Well, let me see if I can cure your husband's madness,' said Philoctetes grimly. 'Where is Odysseus?'

'He started frothing at the mouth this morning,' answered Penelope, 'then he jumped through a window and ran howling to the sea.'

'Take me there,' ordered Philoctetes.

Penelope, still holding her baby, led the way to the beach. There was Odysseus, singing and shouting loudly. He had harnessed two bulls to a plough and was driving them up and down, covering the sand dunes with salt. 'You see,' said Penelope, turning to Philoctetes. 'It is just like I told you. He is mad. Quite mad.'

Philoctetes nodded, but did not answer. He watched Odysseus through narrowed eyes. Then, suddenly, without warning, he grabbed the baby from Penelope's arms and placed him just in front of the bulls. Penelope screamed and rushed forward to try to save her son. But

Odysseus had already steered the bulls to one side. He had also stopped singing and shouting. He dropped the whip. He stared at Philoctetes with hatred.

'Not so mad when your son lies in your path, I see,' said Philoctetes.

'That was a low trick,' answered Odysseus.

'But one that worked. You are no madder than I am, Odysseus. And therefore you are duty bound to obey your oath. You must leave your wife and son and come with me to Troy.'

Odysseus gave a short nod. With his eyes still fixed on Philoctetes, he crossed to Penelope and took her in his arms. He gave her a long kiss. Then he kissed his son. 'Goodbye, my wife,' he whispered. 'Goodbye, my son. I will see you soon, I am sure. And in the meantime, do not think that I will forget who tore me away from you.' And with that, he turned and left with Philoctetes.

The two of them set sail with their men to join Menelaus. Philoctetes, aware of his rival's hatred, never dropped his guard, but Odysseus did nothing. He seemed unhappy and withdrawn. Philoctetes enjoyed his revenge. After all, if he could not have Penelope, then why should anyone else? And why should another prince enjoy the comforts of family and peace when he had neither? Philoctetes was glad that all of Greece was sailing to Troy. He was glad that men and women were being torn apart by war. He was glad that others would share in his loneliness.

And so it was that the poison continued to fester in his heart.

A thousand ships had gathered to sail for Troy. When all stood ready for their departure, there was a great blast of trumpets and the sails filled with wind. The Greek fleet moved out across the sea. Philoctetes and his seven ships were in the front rank. Just behind them was Odysseus. They all made good speed. After two days' of sailing they were getting near to Troy. This was just as well, for the fleet was already running short of water and the Greeks were getting thirsty. Lookouts in every ship began to scan the horizon for land.

Philoctetes spotted the island first. He ordered his ships to change direction and head straight for it. Odysseus and his ships followed close behind, then the rest of the fleet. From a

70

thousand ships, thirsty men plunged into the sea and waded on to the beaches. The island was small and barren, but streams could be heard babbling everywhere, and the water was clear and cool. The Greeks drank until their stomachs swelled. Barrels were filled and stored in the holds of the ships. A few men went hunting in the mountains for goats. Among them was Philoctetes. No one was a better archer. Each time he came back to his ship he brought fresh game with him. The smell of roasting meat filled the air. The men from Odysseus's boats breathed it in. Without telling their captain, they asked if they might share in the feast. When Odysseus saw his men eating as the guests of Philoctetes, he was furious. He reached for his own bow and spent the whole day hunting. When he returned to the beach, he brought enough game to feed both his own and Philoctetes' men – and he did so.

Now it was the turn of Philoctetes to feel insulted. He went into the mountains again: up the winding path he went. Ahead of him he saw a flock of wild goats. He reached for an arrow, drew his bowstring, took a step forwards and aimed the arrow. As he did so, he brought his

71

bare heel down on to the earth. Something crunched beneath it – and Philoctetes felt a sharp stab of pain. He cried out in agony and fell to the ground, clutching his heel. Two trickles of blood were flowing from it, and a horrible smell was rising from the wound. When he looked to see what he had trodden on, he found the body of a snake. It had black diamonds on its back, but otherwise it was red. Its skull had been crushed. Blood and a bright green poison flowed from the pulp.

Using his bow as a crutch, Philoctetes hobbled back to his ships. As he went, he could feel the poison spreading through his blood. The smell from his wound was growing worse by the minute. By the time he reached the beach, it was overpowering. His men could not bear to go near him. Philoctetes fell on to the sand. The other Greeks stood in a circle round him. He sobbed and howled with the pain. He felt dizzy with the stink of the wound and begged for help, but everyone watching him just took a further step away. They all kept their hands clasped over their noses.

All that night, Philoctetes' cries of pain drifted over the beach so that no one could sleep. In the morning, Odysseus spoke to Menelaus and the other Greek leaders. He told them that his men were getting depressed. It was bad for their spirits to have to listen to Philoctetes all night. Even worse was the smell. 'We cannot put up with this,' he said. 'After all, we will soon be at Troy. We have a war to fight.'

The other leaders looked uneasy. Menelaus bit his lip, then said, 'What exactly are you proposing?'

'Leave him here,' answered Odysseus smoothly. 'There is water. There is game. He will hardly starve.'

Again, the other leaders glanced uneasily at one another. There was a long silence. Dimly, above the waves, Philoctetes's cries could be heard. Menelaus looked at the others, then he gave a nod. 'Let's be on our way,' he said. 'Hoist the sails for Troy.'

'Every able-bodied man?' asked Odysseus.

Menelaus inclined his head. 'Naturally. We have no use for anyone who is not well-bodied. As you pointed out, we are going to war.'

So the Greeks went back out to their ships. Even those who had sailed with Philoctetes abandoned their king. The ships pulled away and Philoctetes was left alone on the beach. His sobs of pain mingled with his curses as he shook his fists at the vanishing ships of the Greek fleet. He watched in despair as the last dots disappeared over the horizon, then he screamed at the heavens. The echoes sounded from the mountains before eventually fading away. Philoctetes buried his head in his hands and wept.

A week passed, then a month, then a year. The only human noises that Philoctetes ever heard were his own cries of agony, and the echoes that they made. Sometimes he would see ships passing the island, but they never stopped. Philoctetes often wondered why. Then, one day, he stopped by a clear and still pool, and caught sight of his reflection. He jumped in horror. There was a ghost staring up at him. Its beard and hair were long and tangled. Its eyes were bloodshot. Its clothes were rags. Its heel was still swollen and putrid. Philoctetes turned away and looked out to sea, where he saw a ship. As the sound of his cry reached it, he saw the men on board staring towards the island, and talking among themselves. Then the ship changed course. Philoctetes watched it sail away, then looked back down into the pool. He studied his reflection. 'I have become a ghost,' he whispered. 'I am trapped on an island of the dead.'

After the first year, he lost all track of time. Each day seemed the same. He slept in a cave like a beast. He drank water from a stream. He hunted goats. When he did so, he would remember Heracles's dying words: 'Are you content to remain a goatherd all your life?' Philoctetes wished that he had been. Better to live as a goatherd than to die like this. He cursed his fate. Sometimes he came close to snapping the hero's great bow in half, but he never did. Despite everything, he still loved to trace his fingers along the curve of the wood. He loved the hum of the string when he played it like a lyre. He loved the deadly glint of the arrows' poisoned tips. So he kept his bow secure; he looked after his arrows; and he clung to the hope that he would leave the island one day.

Then, one evening, shortly after sunset, he saw the blaze of a fire on the beach. He stared at it in amazement and his heart started to beat fast. He crept slowly towards it and could make out three men huddled around the flames. A small boat had been dragged up on to the sand. Fishermen, Philoctetes supposed. But why now? What were they doing there? He knew he should be careful, but he was so desperate for human company that he could not help himself. He began shouting and the three men looked round. Using his bow as a crutch, Philoctetes stumbled across the sand until he reached the fire. He fell down on his knees, clasped his hands together and begged the strangers to help him escape. His words made no sense at first because it had been so long since he had spoken to anyone, but at last he made his meaning clear.

The three men, holding their hands to their nostrils, looked unsure. Philoctetes promised them that he was a king. He promised them gold. He almost sobbed as he begged them. At last the three men nodded their heads and said that they would take him away. One of them offered Philoctetes some bread. He fell on it greedily, tearing at it like a dog. It was the first time he had tasted bread for many years. The three men smiled. When Philoctetes had finished eating, they offered him some wine.

He grabbed at the jar eagerly and gulped down the wine. Even as he swallowed it, he could feel the alcohol. The stars, the moon and the sky began to spin. Philoctetes took another swig. Everything spun even more. He moaned and stumbled, then collapsed. The world went black.

When he woke, Philoctetes found that his hands had been tied behind his back. He was tied to a post that had been driven into the sand. A man was sitting opposite him. Philoctetes shook his head in disbelief. The man was the last person in the world he wanted to see: Odysseus.

There was a long silence.

'You need a haircut,' said Odysseus at last.

Philoctetes struggled to his feet and tried to throw himself at his enemy, but the rope that held him to the post yanked him back.

'You see now why I had to tie you up,' said Odysseus. 'But I do regret it. Hear me out, and I will let you go.'

'Why should I believe you?'

Odysseus looked hurt. 'I'm here, aren't I? I've come all this way for you.'

'After leaving me here for . . . for . . .'

'For ten years.'

'*Ten* years?'

Odysseus nodded. 'All a mistake. You see, when we left you here, we did not know what we know now.'

'And what is that?'

Odysseus leaned forward. 'As I said, we have spent ten years camped outside the walls of Troy. Still they won't fall. Why? That question has been worrying me a good deal, as you can imagine. So I decided to find out. I disguised myself as a beggar and crept into Troy. I kidnapped the high priest and took him back to our camp. I demanded to know the secrets of the city's defences. Not the walls, the battlements, boring details like that. No, I wanted to know deeper secrets. Oracles we might have missed. Details of the city's fate that the Trojans knew but we did not. Mysteries revealed to them by the gods.'

Despite himself, Philoctetes was intrigued. 'And what did you find out?'

'That Troy would not fall until a certain condition had been met.'

'Did the high priest reveal the condition to you?'

'Oh, yes.' Odysseus nodded. 'After some "persuasion", yes.'

'And what was it?'

'Ah, well, that is why I am here.' Odysseus reached behind his back and drew out Philoctetes's bow and his quiver of arrows. He studied them, then looked again at Philoctetes. 'We need you to join us,' he said at last. 'We need you to fire the great bow of Heracles in battle. We need you to kill Prince Paris. For you see, until you do that, the walls of Troy can never be brought down.'

Philoctetes laughed, a bitter, hollow laugh. 'You really expect me to help you? You and all the other Greeks who left me here for a decade? You must be mad!'

'Mad?' Now it was Odysseus's turn to laugh. 'Yes. As mad as when you came to fetch me from Ithaca. Which is to say, not at all.'

'Then how can you possibly think that I would come and fight for you?'

Odysseus shrugged. 'Because I know something you do not.'

'Which is?'

Odysseus rose and took a step forward. He stared down at Philoctetes's rotting heel and pulled a face. 'Time hasn't healed your wound, I see.'

Philoctetes did not answer.

'Is it *utter* agony?' asked Odysseus.

'Stop playing games with me.'

'Oh, I am not playing games. You see,' Odysseus paused, 'I know how it can be cured.'

'Liar.' But Philoctetes still felt a sudden surge of hope. 'This is another of your tricks.'

'I can see why you would think so. But I promise you, it is not. And here is the proof. Sail with me now. Leave this island for ever. Come with me to Troy. You will not have to lift your bow in anger until you are healed. We cannot make you fight. Only once you are cured will we ask you to go to battle. Only once you are cured will we ask you to shoot Prince Paris. Only once you are cured will we ask you to slay him with the venom of the hydra's blood.'

Philoctetes remained silent. He lay still where he was and listened to the waves. He looked up at the mountains of the island. Then he turned and gazed eastwards at the horizon, to where Troy lay, beyond the line of the sea and sky.

When Odysseus walked up to him and cut the rope that tied his hands, he rose to his feet. He took his bow and arrows back from his enemy's, and then he hobbled after Odysseus and took his place in the boat.

Yonani stopped.

'Is that it?' gasped Paris. 'Is that the end of your story?'

'There is nothing more to say.'

'So it is the hydra's poison in my blood?'

'It is.'

'It was Philoctetes who shot me?'

'It was.'

'After he had been cured?'

'Yes,' answered Yonani. 'So it seems.'

Paris struggled to sit up. 'But who could have done it? Who had the power to heal his wound?'

Yonani smiled. Her lips tightened. 'Can you not guess?'

Paris did guess. It took him a moment, even with Yonani smiling down at him, but he did finally guess. 'You,' he whispered. 'It was you. Then . . .' He shuddered. He moaned. 'I am doomed. There is no hope.'

81

'No hope at all. Not for you. Nor for me. No hope.'

'Please.'

'No.'

'I beg you.'

'Beg as much as you like. My answer will stay the same. I am the one who killed you, Paris. As surely as if it were my own hand that fired the arrow from Heracles's bow.'

'Why?'

'*Why?* Because you killed me first, Paris.'

He stared at her for a moment longer, then he screamed at his servants: 'Get me away from here! Get me away! Get me away!' The servants picked up the stretcher, but even as they lifted it, Paris began to shake. The fever was more terrible than before. He shrieked in his agony. His words bubbled on flecks of spit. 'Get me away!'

Yonani watched them go. When they had vanished into the trees, she listened to the crashing they made. When that had faded into silence, she rejoiced. She clenched her fists, then raised them in joy. She laughed in triumph, then she listened again to the silence. It closed around her. She imagined it would swallow her up. Then she howled, an animal howl of pain.

'It is not too late,' she told herself. 'It is not too late to correct the mistake I have made.' She began to run through the undergrowth. She moved faster than the fastest deer. 'Paris!' she wailed. 'Paris!' But there was no answer. On she ran. Then, from ahead of her, she heard sobbing and wailing.

Paris had died in the same clearing where Hermes and the three goddesses had appeared to him. Yonani took his body in her arms and covered it in kisses. The heat was still coming from his limbs. She hugged her lover tight to herself and lay with him on the grass. Still the heat radiated from his body.

Meanwhile, the servants had been gathering wood to build the funeral fire. They raised it high. When all was ready, they laid Paris's body on its top, then held a torch to it. The flames leapt up, licked the wood, then began to caress the body of Paris. The smoke turned greasy with his melting flesh. Yonani threw herself upon the flames. She hugged the body of Paris – and she hugged the fire.

But she could not die. And when her lover's

body had burned away, she rose from the ashes of the fire and left the glade, to return to the emptiness of her mountain.

And never did she allow herself to fall in love with a mortal again.

WORLD BOOK DAY
Quick Reads

Quick Reads are published alongside and in partnership with BBC RaW.

We would like to thank all our partners in the *Quick* Reads project for all their help and support:

Department for Education and Skills
Trades Union Congress
The Vital Link
The Reading Agency
National Literacy Trust

Quick Reads would also like to thank the Arts Council England and National Book Tokens for their sponsorship.

We would also like to thank the following companies for providing their services free of charge: SX Composing for typesetting all the titles; Icon Reproduction for text reproduction; Norske Skog, Stora Enso, PMS and Iggusend for paper/board supplies; Mackays of Chatham, Cox and Wyman, Bookmarque, White Quill Press, Concise, Norhaven and GGP for the printing.

www.worldbookday.com

Quick Reads

BOOKS IN THE *Quick* Reads SERIES

Blackwater	Conn Iggulden
The Book Boy	Joanna Trollope
Chickenfeed	Minette Walters
Cleanskin	Val McDermid
Danny Wallace and the Centre of the Universe	Danny Wallace
Desert Claw	Damien Lewis
Don't Make Me Laugh	Patrick Augustus
The Dying Wish	Courttia Newland
The Grey Man	Andy McNab
Hell Island	Matthew Reilly
How to Change Your Life in 7 Steps	John Bird
I Am a Dalek	Gareth Roberts
I Love Football	Hunter Davies
The Name You Once Gave Me	Mike Phillips
The Poison in the Blood	Tom Holland
Screw It, Let's Do It	Richard Branson
Someone Like Me	Tom Holt
Star Sullivan	Maeve Binchy
The Team	Mick Dennis
The Thief	Ruth Rendell
Winner Takes All	John Francome
Woman Walks into a Bar	Rowan Coleman

Look out for more titles in the *Quick* Reads series being published in 2007.

www.worldbookday.com

Have you enjoyed reading this
Quick Reads book?

Would you like to read more?

Or learn how to write fantastically?

If so, you might like to attend a course to
develop your skills.

Courses are **free** and available in your local area.

If you'd like to find out more,
phone **0800 100 900.**

You can also ask for a **free video or DVD** showing
other people who have been on our courses and
the changes they have made in their lives.

Don't get by – get on.

Don't get by get on 0800 100 900

FIRST CHOICE BOOKS

If you enjoyed this book, you'll find more great reads on www.firstchoicebooks.org.uk. First Choice Books allows you to search by type of book, author and title. So, whether you're looking for romance, sport, humour – or whatever turns you on – you'll be able to find other books you'll enjoy.

You can also borrow books from your local library. If you tell them what you've enjoyed, they can recommend other good reads they think you will like.

First Choice is part of The Vital Link, promoting reading for pleasure. To find out more about The Vital Link visit www.vitallink.org.uk

RaW

Find out what the BBC's RaW (Reading and Writing) campaign has to offer at www.bbc.co.uk/raw

NEW ISLAND

New Island publishers have produced four series of books in its Open Door series – brilliant short novels for adults from the cream of Irish writers. Visit www.newisland.ie and go to the Open Door section.

SANDSTONE PRESS

In the Sandstone Vista Series, Sandstone Press Ltd publish quality contemporary fiction and non-fiction books. The full list can be found at their website www.sandstonepress.com.

Quick Reads

The Dying Wish **by Courttia Newland**

Abacus

How do you want to be remembered?

Private investigator Ervine James is feeling
great. Business is booming, and his new partner
Carmen Sinclair is smarter and sharper than he
could ever have hoped. But then, by chance,
he meets a woman with strange eyes, and the
company in the office next door mysteriously
disappears. Soon Ervine is drawn into a
puzzle so deep, so sinister, that the truth could
cost him his life.

Quick Reads

Desert Claw by Damien Lewis

Arrow

In present-day Iraq thieves roam the streets. People are being killed in broad daylight. Security is non-existent. And now, terrorists have seized a Van Gogh painting worth £25 million from one of Saddam's palaces. They are offering it to the highest bidder . . .

Mick Kilbride and his buddy 'East End' Eddie are ex-SAS soldiers. The British Government doesn't want to pay the ransom money to the terrorists. Instead, it hires Mick and his team of ex-Special Forces to get the painting back. Their mission takes them into a dark and violent world where all is not as it seems. And if Mick and Eddie are going to stay alive, they're going to have to stay one step ahead of the enemy . . . and their betrayers.